Dinosaurs, Asteroids,
& Superstars

By Franklyn M. Branley

Color: from Rainbows to Lasers

Comets, Meteoroids, and Asteroids: Mavericks of the Solar
System

The Earth: Planet Number Three

The Electromagnetic Spectrum

Energy for the 21st Century

Experiments in Sky Watching

Experiments in the Principles of Space Travel

Feast or Famine? The Energy Future

Lodestar: Rocket Ship to Mars

Man in Space to the Moon

Mars: Planet Number Four

The Milky Way: Galaxy Number One

The Moon: Earth's Natural Satellite

The Nine Planets

Pieces of Another World: The Story of Moon Rocks

Solar Energy

The Sun: Star Number One

Water for the World

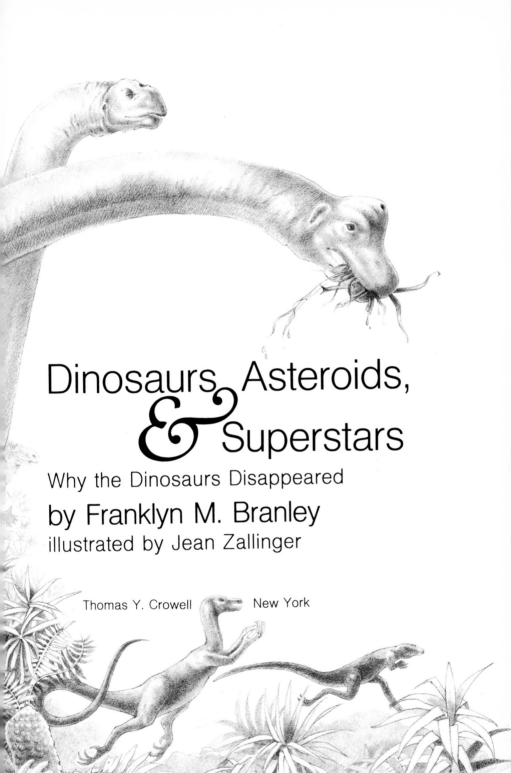

Dinosaurs, Asteroids, & Superstars

Why the Dinosaurs Disappeared

by Franklyn M. Branley
illustrated by Jean Zallinger

Thomas Y. Crowell   New York

Dinosaurs, Asteroids, & Superstars: Why the Dinosaurs Disappeared

Text copyright © 1982 by Franklyn M. Branley
Illustrations copyright © 1982 by Jean Zallinger
For information address
Thomas Y. Crowell Junior Books
10 East 53rd Street
New York, N.Y. 10022.

Published simultaneously in Canada
by Fitzhenry & Whiteside Limited, Toronto.

Library of Congress Cataloging in Publication Data
Branley, Franklyn Mansfield, 1915–
   Dinosaurs, asteroids, and superstars.
   Summary: Discusses possible causes of the sudden
extinction of dinosaurs at the close of the Cretaceous
Period.
   1. Dinosaurs—Juvenile literature. [1. Dinosaurs.
2. Extinct animals] I. Zallinger, Jean, ill. II. Title.
QE862.D5B65   567.9'1   81–43880
ISBN 0–690–04211–6   AACR2
ISBN 0–690–04212–4 (lib. bdg.)

1 2 3 4 5 6 7 8 9 10
First Edition

Contents

Dinosaurs, Asteroids, & Superstars

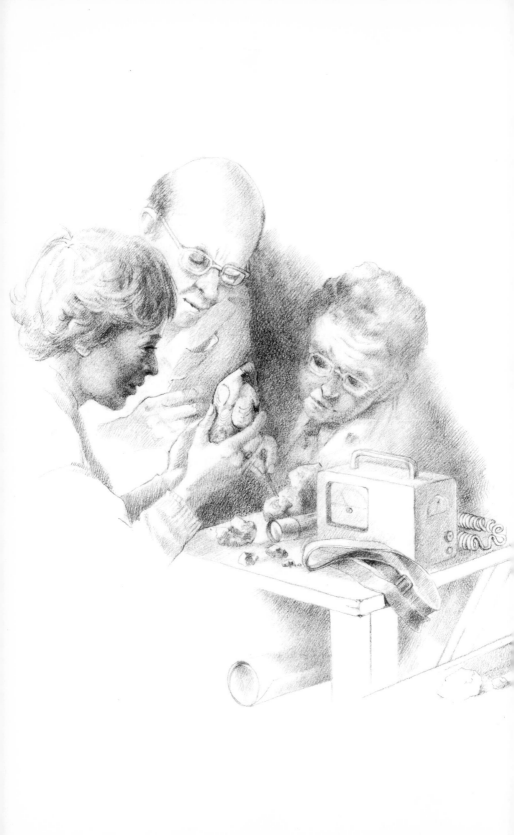

1/
The Dinosaur Puzzle

Dinosaurs first appeared on earth about 205 million years ago. During the next 140 million years, they spread to all parts of the planet. There were many kinds. Fossils of at least 250 different kinds have been found, and no doubt there are many more kinds. Scientists are still finding fossils of new kinds of dinosaurs. (Some people think there may have been 5,000 of them.) And there were large numbers of dinosaurs. They lived in all parts of the world. In many places there were huge

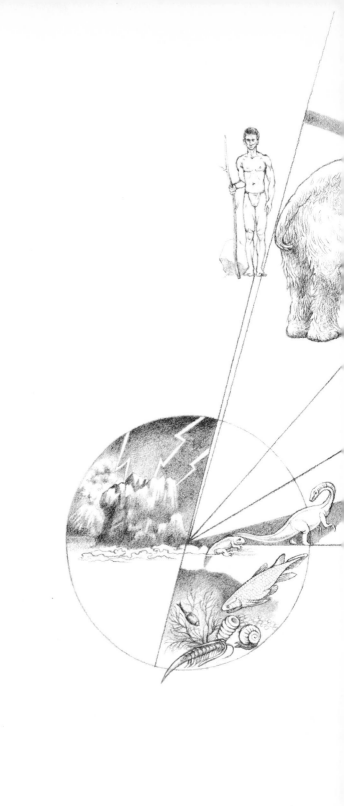

herds of them. Paleontologists, people who study ancient fossils, believe there must have been millions of dinosaurs on the planet. There were large ones and small ones, plant-eaters (herbivores) and meat-eaters (carnivores).

Scientists know when dinosaurs appeared and how long they remained on earth. They can figure out the ages of the layers of rock in which dinosaur fossils are found. One way of doing this depends upon the amount of uranium and lead in the rocks. This is how it works.

Suppose it took a million years for a piece of ice to melt down just halfway. If you had equal amounts of water and ice, you would know that a million years had gone by. In another million years, half the ice that was left would become water. And in another million years, half of *that* ice would change to water. The number of years that had passed could be found by measuring the amount of ice and the amount of water.

Now, scientists know that it takes 700 million years for half of uranium-235 to become lead. In a sample of rock they measure the amount of lead—the kind of lead that uranium changes into—and the amount of uranium. When they know the amounts, they can figure out how long it took the lead to form. That will be the age of the rock, and also the age of the fossils that are found in it.

By dating rocks in this way, or with similar tests, scientists have concluded that the earliest dinosaurs are about 205 million years old. The earth is much older, about 4.5 billion (or 4,500 million) years old. The ages of some other objects and creatures are:

Age of

Sun	4,600 million years
Earth	4,500 million years
Moon	4,500 million years
Oldest dinosaurs	205 million years
Primitive man	4 million years
Modern man	1 million years

Paleontologists divide the history of life on earth into three big parts called eras, which are listed below:

PALEOZOIC is the oldest. The name comes from two Greek words—*paleo,* which means "ancient," and *zoic,* which means "animal life." The Paleozoic Era goes way back to the beginning of the planet.

MESOZOIC is the middle era of animal

life—*meso* means "middle." This was the age of the dinosaurs. It began about 225 million years ago.

CENOZOIC is the present era—*ceno* means "new" or "recent." This is the era when mammals became important. It began about 65 million years ago.

The Mesozoic Era—the time of the dinosaurs— is divided into three parts. The first, and oldest, is called the Triassic Period. The name comes from triad (three), and is used because there are three distinct kinds of rock layers in which fossils of this time are found. The earliest dinosaurs appeared during the Triassic Period.

Somewhat younger is the Jurassic Period. It is named after the Jura Mountains in France. Many fossils of dinosaurs that lived at this time have been found in the Jura Mountains. The Jurassic Period was the time when really huge dinosaurs thrived.

The last part of the Mesozoic Era is called the Cretaceous Period. The name comes from the Latin word *creta,* which means "chalk." Many fossils of this time were found in chalk-like (limestone) rocks.

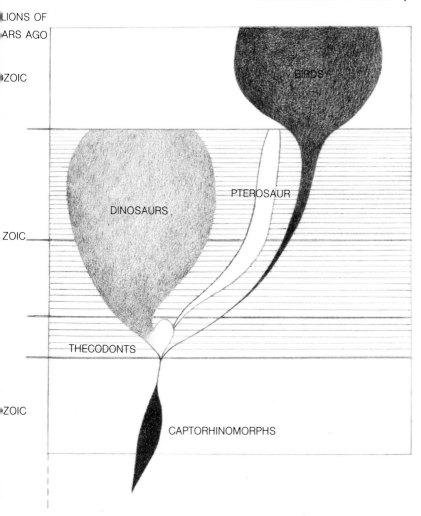

In the chart we show the three eras—Paleozoic, Mesozoic and Cenozoic. Dinosaurs were not the only creatures to appear in the Triassic Period; pterosaurs (flying reptiles) and birds also appeared then. As the centuries passed, the dinosaurs became more widespread, as is shown by the enlargement of their section of the chart.

Long before there were dinosaurs, creatures called captorhinomorphs lived on the earth. These were runty creatures with no necks and short tails. Their legs extended sideways from their bodies and their bellies dragged on the ground, much like the legs and bellies of the crocodiles of today.

Gradually, these runty creatures evolved, and thecodonts became dominant. The thecodonts were fast-moving animals that pushed aside other reptiles. A typical thecodont was Euparkeria (shown in the illustration). The thecodonts were the ancestors of all dinosaurs.

SEYMOURIA

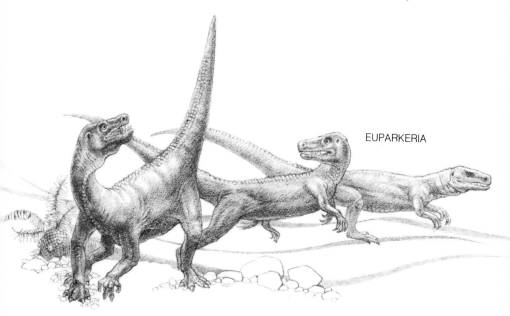

EUPARKERIA

The chart shows a smooth change from one of these creatures to the next. Paleobiologists, people who study ancient life and changes in it, understand how such changes might occur. What they can't understand is the sharp cutoff at the top of the dinosaur section. At the close of the Cretaceous Period, dinosaurs suddenly disappeared; they became extinct. So did pterosaurs, the flying reptiles, and ichthyosaurs, the reptiles that lived in the sea. Why did this happen? How could millions of creatures that had flourished for 140 million years suddenly disappear? That is the puzzle of the dinosaurs. In this book we'll talk about some of the answers that have been suggested.

2/
The Puzzle Gets Harder

Whatever happened 65 million years ago affected the whole world—every continent, and the air and the sea as well as the land. No large land animals remained after the end of the Cretaceous Period; no large air or sea creatures remained, either. And many smaller forms of life also disappeared. No ammonites were left in the deep oceans. (Ammonites were mollusks with tentacles, and were related to squids.) Plankton disappeared from surface waters. (Plankton are tiny plants and ani-

mals that provide food for fish and many whales.) Probably as much as 80 percent of the plants and animals on earth were destroyed. The only living things that remained were mammals, birds, insects, fishes, a few smaller reptiles and a few land plants.

The plants and animals that survived were the ones that had been least prominent during the Mesozoic Era. The ones that had been most prominent were the ones that disappeared. Numerous theories have been proposed to explain what happened.

CAMPTOSAURUS   APATOSAURUS   STEGOSAURUS

Old Age

At one time, paleontologists suggested that dinosaurs as a group had reached old age at the end of the Cretaceous Period. They argued that individuals are born, flourish and then die; why shouldn't whole groups go through the same series of changes? They said that Triceratops was a good example of what they had in mind. This dinosaur had a bony frill, or neck shield, behind its skull, a formation that the scientists considered "abnormal" and the result of "old age" in dinosaurs as a group.

ALLOSAURUS   CERATOSAURUS

This theory never became popular, because the basis of it is false. Although individuals live and die, there is no reason to assume that a group behaves in the same manner. Turtles, for example, were just as old as Triceratops, yet they did not die out.

Poisoning

Two kinds of plants that grew in the early part of the Mesozoic Era were ferns and cycads (lush plants that looked rather like large tree ferns or palm trees). They contained large amounts of tannin, a chemical that could be poisonous to some creatures but that certainly was not harmful to plant-eating dinosaurs, for they ate tons of it.

ANKYLOSAURUS

About 120 million years ago, flowering plants appeared. These plants contained alkaloids, some of which are poisonous. Some scientists wonder if these alkaloids might have killed off the dinosaurs. Perhaps herbivorous dinosaurs ate large quantities of the plants and did not feel the effects of poisoning until it was too late. If large numbers of plant-eaters died, there would be little food for meat-eaters, and they, too, would die.

Many find this theory unacceptable. The flowering plants evolved over millions of years, and dinosaurs ate them for equally long periods. Yet the dinosaurs did not disappear gradually, but suddenly. In fact, with the appearance of flowering plants, dinosaurs flourished. There were vast herds of plant-eating ankylosaurs (armored dinosaurs) and ceratopsians (horned dinosaurs). And as plant-eaters flourished, so did the meat-eating dinosaurs that preyed on them.

Even if some such poisoning killed off dinosaurs, the theory does not explain why pterosaurs disappeared from the skies, and ichthyosaurs from the seas.

Widespread Disease

It is possible for a single kind of animal to become

sick, and for the sickness to become widespread. In the present day, for example, cows occasionally get hoof-and-mouth disease. The sickness can spread very rapidly across wide areas, and unless it is stopped, it will wipe out tremendous numbers of cows.

Perhaps some sort of disease spread around the world and wiped out the dinosaurs. It might have been one that did not affect mammals, insects, small reptiles, birds and fish.

We must remember, however, that dinosaurs were not the only creatures to disappear at the end of the Cretaceous Period. The disease theory does not explain why 80 percent of life on the planet died off.

The Question of Eggs

Although there were dinosaurs that gave birth to living young, most baby dinosaurs came from eggs. Dinosaurs did not hatch their eggs the way birds and chickens do. A chicken first builds a nest. Then eggs are laid in the nest, one a day for the next two weeks or so. The hen sits on the eggs, keeping them warm until the chicks break through the shell. Once they are hatched, the chicks are guarded from attacks by birds, animals, and other hazards. Because of the care provided by the mother hen, a good many of the chicks survive.

Dinosaurs were indifferent mothers. They dug shallow holes and laid eggs in layers, one atop the other. Once the eggs were laid down, the layers were covered with a thin layer of soil.

The eggs were not cared for at all. After they were laid and covered, the adult dinosaurs went their way. Once the young dinosaurs had worked their way out of the shells, they had to survive on their own. The adults were not around to protect them.

Pretty much the same thing happens today with green turtles. At high tide they dig a hole in the sand at the edge of the waterline, and lay their eggs. The nest is covered with sand, and the turtle goes back to the sea. She never returns. Egg hunters eat many of the eggs. The baby turtles that hatch from the surviving eggs must make their way to the sea, hopefully lasting long enough to get there and swim away.

Very likely, a good many of the dinosaur eggs never hatched. They were eaten by other dinosaurs that happened to discover the nest. Also at that time there were many small mammals that had large brains compared to their body size. This meant they used their wits in order to survive. Dinosaurs would have stumbled on the eggs, but these brainy mammals would have searched them out. Very likely one of their favorite foods was dinosaur eggs. They would have uncovered the nests, broken open the eggs, and would have eaten the contents.

You would also expect that, once hatched, only a few of the young dinosaurs would survive. However, enough of them did survive to renew the dinosaur population for 140 million years. Both the eggs and the young dinosaurs might have been vulnerable to predators. But paleontologists do not think this would account for the complete disappearance of the dinosaurs. Certainly it would not explain the disappearance of the ichthyosaurs, the sea reptiles that gave birth in the water to living young. Something else must have been going on.

Now, fossil dinosaur eggs have been found at various locations around the world. Eggs from older rock layers have thick shells—as thick as ten or 20 pages of this book. Those found in younger rock layers have thinner shells, and the eggs in the youngest layers have the thinnest shells of all. The shells of these youngest eggs are less than half as thick as the shells of eggs in the older layers. And many of the eggs that have been found in the youngest layers are whole. In other words, they never hatched.

Very likely this means that the later dinosaurs were under some sort of stress. The same thing happens today to the eggs of birds if the birds are very cold, if they are starving or if they absorb certain chemicals from their food. Their eggs become thin-shelled—so thin-shelled they would break as the young birds developed. But the young birds do not develop properly. Their bones may lack calcium (an embryo bird gets calcium from the shell of its egg), so the bones lack strength. Many birds do not hatch. Also, those that do hatch often have crooked legs, undeveloped wings or other formations that make it impossible for them to survive.

It seems that the dinosaurs had a very difficult time toward the end of the Cretaceous Period. Whatever happened, it caused the dinosaurs to lay eggs with shells so thin that young dinosaurs could not hatch from them.

Obviously, if no new young animals were hatched, it wouldn't take long for the entire dinosaur population to die out. But, again, we must remember that the dinosaurs were not the only form of life to vanish at the end of the Cretaceous Period. Again we must ask, what could have caused so very many different living things to die out all at the same time?

Plankton and pollen grains may give part of the answer.

Clues from Plankton

Plankton are single-celled plants or animals that are inside tiny hard shells. They flourish in seawater. Fossils of the shells of plankton have been found in rock formations that are millions of years old. By carefully studying the plankton fossils, scientists have learned a lot about conditions in the ancient oceans.

Plankton fossils show that a very sharp change occurred at the end of the Mesozoic Era and the beginning of the Cenozoic. For one thing, the plankton of the early Cenozoic Era are much smaller than the plankton of the late Mesozoic. This implies that the temperature of the seas suddenly dipped much lower. Plankton of the Mesozoic Era were heat-loving; in warm tropical seas they grew quite large. There must have been severe changes in climate that destroyed these "tropical" plankton along with the dinosaurs. Those few plankton that survived gradually adjusted to the colder water. From them new and different types evolved.

CYCAD

Clues from Pollen Grains

Pollen grains are durable parts of plants. Deposits of them in rock formations are clues to the kinds of plants that existed at the close of the Mesozoic Era. Scientists have found that at that time, at least half of the plants were tropical—they needed heat to survive. But fossil pollen shows that by the early Cenozoic, only a third of the plants required warm temperatures all year round. Evergreens were taking over, for they can survive severe weather changes. (Needles are much less sensitive to cold weather than leaves are.)

A principal food of plant-eating dinosaurs was cycads. Cycads needed high temperatures both day and night, and all through the year. Apparently these plants disappeared abruptly, which indicates that earth cooled suddenly—at least, there must have been periods of severe cold at some time during a yearly cycle.

Why Mammals Survived

At the same time that dinosaurs lived, small mammals lived upon earth. The largest of these was no larger than a cat. As we have said, mammals survived the changes that killed the dinosaurs. This might be explained by differences between dinosaurs and the mammals of the time.

Dinosaurs may have become too big and specialized. Perhaps, as conditions on earth changed, the dinosaurs were unable to adapt to them. Small mammals were more able to adapt because they

could live in various environments, and they could survive on various kinds of food. And mammals had hair or fur to keep them warm during cold weather.

Now, it has long been thought that the dinosaurs were reptiles. Large reptiles cannot endure cold weather, because they are cold-blooded. This means that their body temperature becomes the same as the temperature of their surroundings. If the weather were cold for a long time, a large reptile's body temperature would get so low that the creature could not function. And it would be too hard for the creature to dig itself a hole, or find some other warm, protected place to stay during cold weather.

On the other hand, small reptiles, such as lizards, can survive cold weather because they can dig holes or burrow into mud, and spend winters underground. Today, small reptiles are found as far north as Canada. But large reptiles, such as alligators, do not live much farther north than Florida, Alabama and southern Georgia.

So, if the dinosaurs were large reptiles, they could not have survived cold winters. But their small relatives—lizards, snakes and turtles—could survive because of their size. Mammals were protected by hair or fur, and birds had feathers to

keep them warm. If the world suddenly became colder, it would explain why the dinosaurs died off, while mammals and a few other small creatures managed to survive.

What if the dinosaurs were warm-blooded, as some scientists now think? Even then they could not have survived a long cold spell. Warm-blooded creatures use the food they eat as fuel to keep them warm. Being large, dinosaurs would have had to eat huge amounts of food. But they could not hold heat in their bodies because they had no hair, fur or feathers. Even if they ate and ate and ate during a cold spell, they would get colder and colder—

cold enough to die.

The best evidence all points to one conclusion: there was a severe change in weather around the world at the end of the Cretaceous Period. The change occurred so abruptly that many plants and animals could not adapt to it.

Some believe this change occurred in less than a million years—not a very long period, given the billions of years of earth's history. Others believe the change might have required only a few thousand years. And some people believe the change occurred in just a few days—although this seems unlikely to many scientists. In any case, such a dramatic change in weather would have killed the

dinosaurs, plesiosaurs, ichthyosaurs and ptero-saurs. All of these creatures thrived in warm weather, and they could not have adjusted to long, cold winters.

Have we solved the puzzle of the dinosaurs, then? Not quite. We still don't know what caused the severe change in weather. (We don't even know for sure that a change in weather is what killed the dinosaurs.) All we know is that the change must have been worldwide, because dino-saurs disappeared from every continent. And the change must have been sudden, because so few plants and animals were able to adapt to it. Some kind of catastrophe must have occurred.

3/
Changing Continents

When dinosaurs first appeared, the continents were not separate, as they are now. During the time that dinosaurs flourished, the continents slowly became separate land masses. Yes, whole continents moved. (Indeed, they are still moving today.) Some land masses moved closer together, others moved farther apart. No doubt such tremendous changes in the face of the earth also changed the destiny of the dinosaurs.

Two hundred million years ago, the land masses

of earth were joined together in one single giant continent. It has been called Pangaea, meaning "all the land." It was an island in a vast super-ocean that is called Panthalassa, meaning "all the sea." An arm of the ocean that extended into this mammoth land mass is called the Tethys Sea. Pangaea covered about 40 percent of the earth's surface—just about the same amount presently covered by the seven continents.

Pangaea was atop semi-molten rock, just as the continents are today. Movements of the semi-molten material caused the land mass to break up.

Once the supercontinent had broken up, the pieces started to move. Probably more movements of the semi-molten material, plus earth's rotation, caused this. At any rate, the motion has persisted for millions of years. The continents are still moving, and, in places, pieces are breaking apart from them. In some places the movement amounts to one centimeter a year. That may not seem like very much, but in a million years it amounts to ten kilometers. (And a million years is quite a short time in the history of the earth.) Other continents move faster. For example, modern measuring methods show that in a lifetime of about 75 years North America moves *two meters* westward!

By about 180 million years ago, Pangaea had

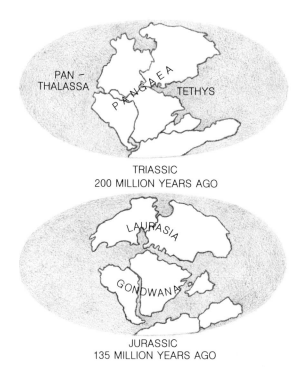

TRIASSIC
200 MILLION YEARS AGO

JURASSIC
135 MILLION YEARS AGO

broken into two distinct sections, a northern one
and a southern one. The northern region, which
is called Laurasia, included what is now North
America, Europe and Asia. The southern region,
which is called Gondwana or Gondwanaland, included what is now South America, Africa, Antarctica, Australia and India.

As you can see from the map, North America
had separated from South America, and the Atlantic Ocean was beginning to form. India had separated from Antarctica, and was drifting northward

toward Laurasia. The land section that was to become Australia was still fastened to Antarctica.

During these early stages in the evolution of the continents, dinosaurs could roam from one part of the world to another. No doubt they ranged far and wide, always in search of more lush plant growth. And as the plant-eaters roamed, the meat-eaters followed along.

When the theory of continental drift was first put forward, many scientists pooh-poohed it. But today, the theory is widely accepted. There is plenty of evidence to show that the continents formed and moved in the manner just described. The same rock formations have been found on "matching" edges of continents—for example, on the east coast of South America (at its "bulge") and the west coast of Africa (where it curves inward). Magnetic patterns in rocks show that the continents of today must once have been in different positions on the globe. And fossils of the same prehistoric animals have been discovered on land masses that are now widely separated.

Fossils of Lystrosaurus, a prehistoric reptile about the size of a large dog, provide important evidence. This creature lived some 200 million years ago. It was short and stocky, with a flat face—

it had no nose at all. Its eyes were high on the head, and it had two short tusks.

Lystrosaurus was not uncommon, for remains of it have been found at many locations in India, China and South Africa. But in 1969 scientists made an uncommon discovery—they found remains of Lystrosaurus at Coalsack Bluff in Antarctica.

Paleontologists knew that Lystrosaurus was a land animal that could not have crossed the sea that now separates Africa from Antarctica. The only way Lystrosaurus could have reached Antarctica was to go overland. This meant that Antarctica must have been connected to Africa, India or China (or all three) at the time that Lystrosaurus lived. Lystrosaurus—short, runty and not at all impressive as prehistoric creatures go—became an important key to the early geography of our planet.

By 135 million years ago, at the end of the Jurassic Period, the land masses of South America and Africa had separated. The sea moved into the break, and so the South Atlantic Ocean began. Eurasia was swinging about, as is shown by the arrows, so the Tethys Sea was closing. India continued to move northward toward Laurasia. Australia was still connected to Antarctica.

Sixty-five million years ago, at the end of the Cretaceous Period, South America and Africa had moved farther apart, and the Atlantic Ocean had become greatly enlarged. India had swung about somewhat. Australia still remained attached to Antarctica.

Land bridges, connections between one part of the world and another, were disappearing. This meant that the migration paths of the dinosaurs were becoming limited. The creatures could move about, but usually only within their own continent.

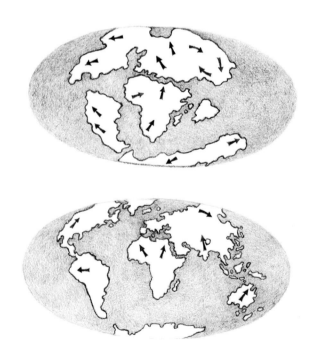

They probably tended to congregate in the warmer regions, where ferns, palms and cycads—the principal foods of the plant-eaters—would have grown most readily. As the plant-eaters migrated, so did the carnivorous dinosaurs that preyed upon them.

Since the Cenozoic Era began, about 65 million years ago, the continents have continued to drift. The western continents are now farther away from those in the eastern part of the world. North America is completely separate from Eurasia. The Arabian peninsula has broken almost entirely free from Africa. Australia has become a separate land mass. And India has pushed into Asia. When the two land masses collided, the Himalayan Mountains were pushed up.

Scientists now believe that the hard outer layer of the earth is divided into several different sections, called plates. It is these plates that actually move, carrying the continents with them. The movements are called plate tectonics—tectonics comes from a Greek word meaning "making" or "building."

Today, the plates of earth are moving in the directions indicated by the arrows. It is believed that 50 million years from now the plates will have carried the continents to quite new locations.

North and South America will have moved westward, while Africa and Eurasia will have moved to the east, so the Atlantic Ocean will be much wider than it is now. Australia will have moved much farther north; it will be starting to push into Asia. Los Angeles and Lower California will have broken free from the continent and will be moving northward toward the Aleutian Islands. (Scientists estimate that in ten million years Los Angeles will be alongside San Francisco.)

During the Mesozoic Era, when the continents were first forming, there must have been terrible earthquakes and violent volcanic action. Weather patterns must have been disrupted, and probably these patterns changed dramatically. Lush tropical areas may have become deserts. And heavy rains may have fallen in regions that had been parched. No doubt there was severe flooding, followed after some time by renewed growth.

All in all, the dinosaurs must have had a rough time. But although the changes produced by tectonics were great and in many cases severe, they were usually gradual, spread over millions of years. They did not bring about the disappearance of the dinosaurs. In fact, the dinosaurs flourished during the very era when major tectonic changes were taking place.

Now, adverse changes in weather and geography would certainly have caused the dinosaurs to migrate. But migrating would have helped the dinosaurs; it would have taken them from unsuitable habitats to better ones. Local changes in weather and landscape could not have killed off all the dinosaurs. As we saw in the last chapter, the disappearance of the dinosaurs can only be explained by a change that was severe, sudden and worldwide.

Perhaps, as some scientists suggest, there was a time when plates collided and joined together in such a way that the Arctic Ocean was cut off from the rest of the world's oceans. Over a long period of time, fresh rainwater would have drained into the blocked-off sea; the Arctic seawater would have become fresher and fresher. Then,

about 65 million years ago—so the theory goes—
an opening to the world's oceans was created when
Greenland and Norway began to pull apart. The
cold, fresh Arctic water poured into the larger
oceans and, being less dense, remained atop the
warmer salt water. The temperature of the warm
salt seas could have dropped by as much as 20
degrees Celsius. That would be enough to kill off
a great many sea plants and animals. And the
cooler water would have evaporated more slowly,
so there would have been a marked decrease in
rainfall. The decrease might have been sharp
enough to cause severe droughts all over the world.
That could have killed the dinosaurs as well as
many other life forms.

This theory sounds logical enough. However,
there is no evidence that the Arctic Ocean was
ever filled with fresh water, or even brackish
(slightly salty) water.

Another theory, and one for which there seems
to be evidence such as changes in rock layers that
formed under the sea, suggests that there was a
rather sudden drop of 60 to 90 meters in the level
of the sea. This would have caused marshy areas
to dry up. A good many dinosaurs lived in such
swampy regions, and an even larger number de-
pended upon swamp plants for their food—either

directly (if they were plant-eaters) or indirectly (if they were meat-eaters).

The thing that caused the dinosaurs to disappear could have been related to tectonics. If it was, the cause of their disappearance was a terrestrial event—terrestrial means "of the earth." But the cause might have been an extraterrestrial event—something that happened outside the earth, in space. Let us look at that possibility.

4/
Superstars

It is possible for events that occur far, far out in space to have a profound effect upon the earth. If such an event occurred 65 million years ago, its effects might have been severe enough to destroy the dinosaurs in a matter of a few months or even days.

The most powerful of all extraterrestrial events is the explosion of a large star—a supernova. Stars vary greatly in size. The sun is a medium-sized star. There are stars thousands of times larger and

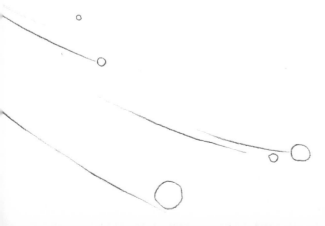

millions of times brighter. (We don't see them as bright objects in the sky because they are very far away.) A very large, bright star is unstable. When it becomes unable to hold itself together, such a superstar explodes. During the explosion, as much as half of the star may blow away. And tremendous amounts of energy will be released. The blast will be equal to the one that would be caused by the explosion of millions of ten-million-ton hydrogen bombs. (Someone has figured out that the explosion of a star about ten times the size of the sun would produce a blast greater than 1×10^{27} times that of a ten-million-ton bomb.)

In the year 1054, the Chinese saw the explosion of just such a star. Looking between the horns of Taurus, the Bull, they saw a star that had not been seen before. They thought it was a new star—a *nova* in Latin. Because it was especially brilliant—according to some reports, it was bright enough to be seen in the daytime—it was called a super-nova.

The "new star" was seen for several weeks; then it faded. Today, we know that what the Chinese saw was the explosion of a large star. The name "supernova" now refers to this kind of explosion.

The gases given off by this particular supernova

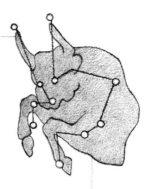

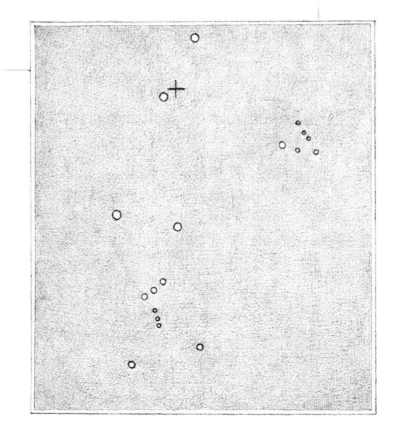

are still visible with a telescope. They make a spectacular formation called the Crab Nebula. The gases are still moving apart at speeds of 1,000 kilometers per second.

Even without a telescope you can find the location of the Crab Nebula. In the winter skies look toward Taurus, which is northwest of Orion, the Hunter. Extending out from Aldebaran, the mightiest star in Taurus, are the horns of the bull, which terminate at two bright stars—Beta and Zeta Tauri. The Crab Nebula is located just above Zeta—that's the dimmer of the two stars.

As we have said, a star gives off tremendous amounts of energy when it explodes. Some of this energy is in the form of brilliant light. The rest of the energy is in the form of heat, X rays and gamma rays.

In 1054, the Chinese experienced only the light from the supernova, because it occurred 5,000 light years away from earth. In other words, the star had exploded 5,000 years earlier and the Chinese were seeing light that had been traveling through space during those 5,000 years. Because of the distance, much of the energy of the explosion was diluted, so it did not affect earth or life upon it.

Supernovas occur at the rate of about three in

a century. Fortunately for us, most of them are very far away. If a supernova were only 100 light years from us, the effects on earth could be disastrous. Radiation throughout earth's atmosphere would increase ten million times—the effect would be equal to that of the explosion of 100,000 nuclear bombs all around the world. Most creatures exposed to such radiation would be killed outright. Or, if they survived, they would produce offspring that were abnormal. Such mutant creatures very likely would not be able to survive.

Perhaps a nearby superstar exploded 65 million years ago and deadly radiation rained down upon earth. This would certainly explain the disappearance of the dinosaurs. But why, then, did mammals and some other small creatures survive? Scientists have a good answer for this: the small creatures could burrow into the ground, where they would be protected from radiation. Dinosaurs could not, so they died.

The supernova theory looks good so far. But there is a problem. Life in the seas would have been protected from radiation by the water—yet much sea life died out. For this reason, some scientists feel that direct bombardment by radiation particles could not have killed the dinosaurs. They believe that radiation affected the atmosphere so that there were drastic changes in conditions on earth.

Perhaps, as energy reached earth from the supernova, much of it was changed into X rays by the atmosphere. If that happened, the X rays would mostly be absorbed by the ozone gas in the upper atmosphere. But the X rays might release large amounts of heat, and this heat would reach earth's surface. This in turn would cause severe updrafts, which would carry tremendous amounts of water vapor to high altitudes. Once there, the water vapor would freeze into ice crystals. These crystals would be numerous enough to act as mirrors that would reflect sunlight out into space. In other words, the ice crystals would prevent sunlight from reaching earth's surface. You can imagine what would happen. Temperatures would drop steeply after only a few days without sunshine.

Plants and creatures of all kinds that were not destroyed by gamma rays from the supernova would surely die from the intense cold. The low temperatures would have lasted long enough to chill the oceans and so destroy much sea life, both plants and animals. However, if such chilling did occur, it did not continue long enough for ice sheets to form on the continents, for geologists find no evidence that there were glaciers during this period of earth's history.

If a supernova *was* somehow responsible for killing off the dinosaurs, the creatures would have disappeared rapidly, and many kinds would have vanished at essentially the same time. Here we see another problem with the supernova theory. The fossil record seems to indicate that the disappearance, though sudden in one sense, was not *that* sudden. It seems that different kinds of dinosaurs gradually died out, until Triceratops and Tyrannosaurus were the main kinds left. Fossils of these two dinosaurs are often found in rocks from the very end of the Cretaceous Period.

Perhaps these creatures were better able to withstand radiation and very cold temperatures. Or perhaps it's not really true that these two kinds of dinosaurs outlived all the others. Only small parts of the rock layers that contain fossils have been explored. It may turn out, when more fossils are found, that many kinds of dinosaurs did die at the very same time.

On the other hand, it may just be that it was *not* a supernova that caused the disappearance of the dinosaurs. Some other event might have been responsible.

5/
Encounter with an Asteroid

A few years ago, scientists were studying rock layers near Gubbio, a small town in Italy. Quite by accident they discovered a thin layer of clay laid down at the end of the Cretaceous Period. The layer contained an extremely large amount of iridium. This is a metal that is very rare on earth, but is quite common in meteoroids and asteroids. From this discovery grew the asteroid-collision theory of the extinction of the dinosaurs.

Asteroids are space objects made up of stone,

metal or metal and stone together. They may be several hundred kilometers across, and they move in orbits. The asteroids as a group make a band or belt located between the orbits of Mars and Jupiter. When seen through a telescope, asteroids look like points of light—that is, like stars. The word asteroid means "star-like."

Frequently an asteroid will move closer to Mars or Jupiter. After this happens many times, the asteroid's orbit may be changed enough that the asteroid swings through the inner solar system. It may cross the orbit of Earth on its way around the sun. It would be possible for such an asteroid to collide with the earth, because the two bodies just might reach the same place in space at the very same time.

In 1972 that almost happened. A small asteroid, perhaps with a diameter of eight or ten meters and a weight of 100 to 1,000 tons, came within 52 kilometers of earth's surface. People in Utah, Idaho and Montana and all the way into Canada saw it as a bright object streaking northward in the afternoon sky. The asteroid grazed earth's upper atmosphere and then skipped off into space, much as a flat stone skips across the water. We are very lucky that this asteroid did not score a direct hit on earth's suface.

Astronomers tell us that this small asteroid travels in a flat ellipse, taking 21½ months to complete one journey around the sun. In 1997 the asteroid and earth will again be at nearly the same position in space. According to astronomers' calculations, the asteroid will reach the position four days before we do, so once again it will miss us. But there's a big "if." Scientists are not certain exactly when the asteroid will cross our orbit—there is an eight-day leeway. So the asteroid could reach the location as much as 12 days before we do, or four days after—or at any time in between. This means there is a chance, though a slim one, that earth and the

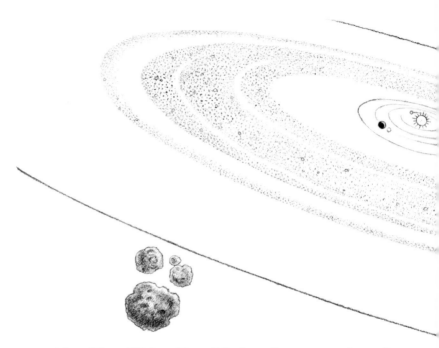

asteroid will collide. Should that happen, the effects would be disastrous. The asteroid packs more wallop than a score of powerful nuclear bombs, and the devastation would be unbelievable if it fell anywhere near a center of population.

Possibly by that time our space agency will have a space-watch operation, with telescopes constantly scanning the sky for unusual objects. If there was a sighting, spacecraft equipped with powerful bombs would be sent to blow up the object before it came close enough to endanger the earth.

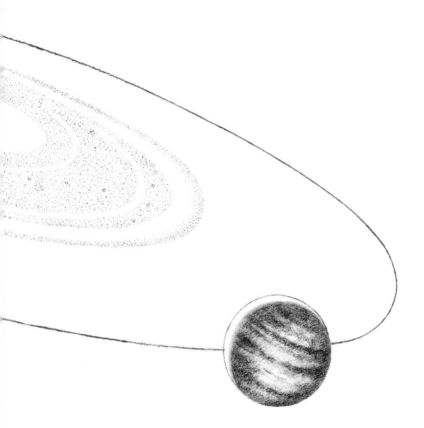

    While the asteroid missed us in 1972, there have been occasions when asteroids—or meteoroids, which are small asteroids—have struck the planet and gouged out tremendous craters. Perhaps the most famous crater is the Canyon Diablo crater near Winslow, Arizona. It is 220 meters deep and

1,200 meters in diameter. In places the wall of the crater is 30 meters above the level of the surrounding countryside. The meteoroid that dug the crater probably crashed into earth some 30,000 years ago.

Now, the layer of iridium-rich clay found at Gubbio, Italy, suggests that an asteroid struck the earth 65 million years ago. If this happened, we would not expect to find a crater today. During all those years, wind and water would have eroded the crater and filled it in. But the crater, if crater there was, would have been simply huge. The scientists who think an asteroid struck earth 65 million years ago say the asteroid must have been over nine kilometers in diameter. It would have made a crater 150 kilometers across! (Astronomers estimate that an asteroid of this size collides with earth once in every 100 million years.)

The asteroid might have been going 100,000 kilometers per hour, and it would have had the energy of 100 trillion tons of dynamite. On impact, the asteroid would have been pulverized, and quadrillions of tons of dust and dirt would have been thrown into the atmosphere. Winds would have carried the dust all around the world. The dust would have formed such a dense layer around the earth that no sunlight could get through.

In the last chapter, we saw what would happen if no sunlight reached earth's surface. Temperatures would drop immediately, and many plants and animals would freeze to death. A dust layer caused by collision with an asteroid could have remained in the atmosphere for five years or more—long enough for world temperatures to drop below freezing. And the dust layer could have affected life in other ways, too. It might have equalized temperatures worldwide. In that case, weather would have been eliminated, for weather occurs because of variations in temperature. The cycle of rainfall would have ended, and fresh water would have disappeared from swamps, lakes and ponds. Plants and animals might have died from lack of water if they didn't freeze to death.

Obviously, if an asteroid did strike earth 65 million years ago, it explains why the dinosaurs sud-

denly vanished. But why, you may wonder, does the iridium in the clay layer at Gubbio lead scientists to think that this is what happened?

As we have said, iridium is very rare on earth. Geologists do not expect to find large amounts of it while they are studying rock formations. Also, iridium is quite common in meteoroids and asteroids. The belief is that asteroids are chunks of the original material from which the planets were formed. As the planets formed, the iridium in them became concentrated in the planets' cores, along with iron. In asteroids there has been no such concentrating process, so the iridium occurs at the surface of those objects. If an asteroid struck the earth and was pulverized, it would be quite natural for there to be a lot of iridium in the dust that finally settled to earth.

Now, if the iridium had been found only in Italy, scientists might have explained its occurrence in some other way. They might have looked for some local cause for the unusual deposits. But the clay-and-iridium layer was found in other places—in Denmark, in New Zealand, in Spain and in cores taken from the bottom of the northern Pacific Ocean. It was logical to conclude that all the deposits were the result of one single worldwide event. That event might very well have been a collision with an asteroid.

As sensible as the asteroid-collision theory may sound, many scientists disagree with it. They may agree that a layer of dust hung in the atmosphere, and that this had disastrous effects. But they don't think the dust was raised by a collision with an asteroid. Let's look at yet another theory about what killed the dinosaurs. . . .

6/
Volcanoes

In the last two chapters, we talked about some really dramatic events that might have affected earth 65 million years ago. You might not think that volcanoes could affect life on earth the way a supernova could, or a collision with an asteroid. But some scientists think it was volcanic activity that led to the disappearance of the dinosaurs.

Certainly we know that there was widespread volcanic activity during the early history of the earth. Movements of plates would have been cause

enough for volcanoes to erupt all around the world. But volcanic eruptions could not have killed every single dinosaur outright. If volcanoes caused the extinction of the dinosaurs, they did so indirectly.

Recently, Mount St. Helens erupted in the state of Washington. Although a third of the mountain was blown into the air as volcanic ash, the eruption was a small one. Yet traces of the ash were found around the world. Fortunately, the ash layer in the air was not dense enough to blot out the sun, so there was no apparent drop in worldwide temperature.

However, in 1815 there was an eruption that did affect temperatures all around the world. Mount Tambora, a volcano in Indonesia, blew its top. Billions of tons of rock were turned into ash and dust and thrown into the air. Winds carried the ash all around the world. The ash clouds were so thick that they filtered out sunshine, and the whole earth got colder and colder. One year later, in 1816, New England had six inches of snow in June, and there were frosts in July and August; 1816 was called the year without a summer. Had the dust and ash remained in the air, earth would have gotten even colder—perhaps cold enough to kill many plants and animals.

Tambora was a big volcano. But it was very

small when compared to the volcanoes that used to exist on our planet. In Sumatra, for example, there is a low region some 100 kilometers across—the remains of what was once a huge volcano. Similar remains of Tambora would be only a few kilometers in diameter.

If Mount Tambora could cause "the year without a summer," you can imagine what a really gigantic volcano—or several of them—could do. The dust and ash thrown into the air by such a huge volcano might blot out the sun almost completely. Temperatures could drop low enough to freeze both plants and animals. (Incidentally, huge volcanoes might have been the source of the iridium deposits found at Gubbio, Italy, and elsewhere. The volcanic ash might have had iridium in it.)

You will remember that not all plants and animals were destroyed at the end of the Cretaceous Period. All the dinosaurs were, of course, and so were all the large flying reptiles (the pterosaurs) and all the large marine reptiles. Now we must ask this question: if the whole earth froze, why didn't *all* life disappear?

Indeed, why not? One logical answer is that the whole earth did *not* freeze. Perhaps a dense layer of dust did surround the earth at the end of the Cretaceous Period. But it might not have blanketed

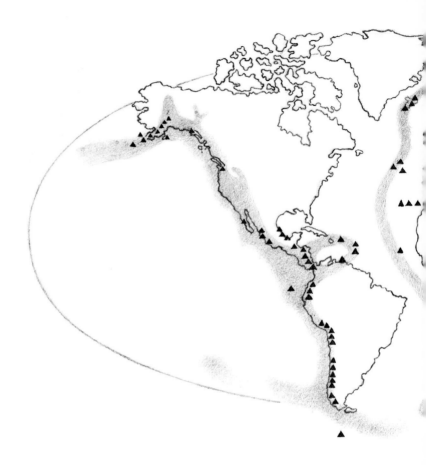

the entire planet. It may have formed into a wide
ring around the earth—a ring not unlike the rings
of Saturn.

7/
A Ring Around the Earth

Scientists who support the "ring" theory of the extinction of the dinosaurs believe that the entire earth did *not* get colder and colder at the end of the Cretaceous Period. Rather, they say, there were seasonal changes. Summers were warm, but winters were severely cold—much colder than they are today—and the severe winter cold hit a much larger region. Such a weather pattern could have been caused by a ring of dense clouds of ash around the earth's equator.

Let's look at what would happen in the northern hemisphere. For part of the year, the sun would be north of the equator, and so north of the ring of dense clouds. Then the weather would be warm and summery, because the ring of clouds would not filter out sunlight. But for much of the year the earth would be tilted differently, and then the dense clouds would keep sunshine from getting to the northern half of the world. The weather would be bitterly cold.

The southern hemisphere would have the same kind of weather, of course, except that it would

be summer there when it was winter in the northern hemisphere—just as it is today.

Only certain kinds of plants and animals could live through such long, severe winters. Animals would have to have hair, fur or feathers to keep them warm or they would have to be small enough to burrow into shelters—or both. And plants would die unless they could withstand subfreezing temperatures. As we saw in chapter 2, dinosaurs could not possibly survive such cold weather.

So, a ring of dense clouds around the earth could have caused the death of all the dinosaurs, and

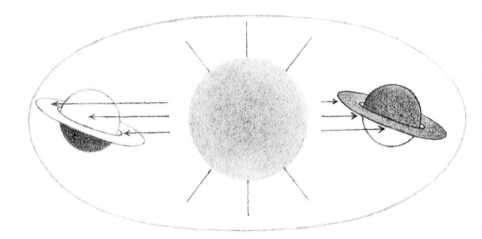

of other warmth-loving creatures and plants as well. But small mammals and a few other small life forms could have survived; so could a few hardy plants.

The dinosaurs might not all have died during the first long, cold winter. Some might have managed to survive from one summer to the next. But, eventually, the severe winter weather would have killed them all.

From earth the ring of clouds would have been impressive. During the day it probably would not have been visible because of the brightness of the sky. At night, however, the particles making up the clouds would have reflected sunlight, just as the moon does. The ring would have made a bright band reaching across the sky from horizon to horizon, shining as brilliantly as a thousand full moons.

Many people who believe in the "ring" theory assume that the ring of clouds was formed from dust particles raised by a collision with an asteroid, or from dust and ash particles thrown up by volcanoes. But some people think that the particles that made up the ring came from the moon. According to their idea, there were violent volcanic eruptions on the moon. (This idea makes sense, because there are many large extinct volcanoes on the moon.) The volcanoes erupted with such violence that ashes were thrown way out into space—so the theory goes—and some were moving fast enough to escape from the moon's gravitational field. They went into orbit around the sun, and later were intercepted by the earth and captured in our own gravitational field.

If this happened, it is likely that some of the particles were pulled down to earth's surface. As they speeded in, they would have made a spectacular display, not unlike a meteor shower. But most of the ash particles, or pellets, would have remained in the atmosphere. There they would have formed into the dense clouds that made up the ring.

There may have been sources of lunar dust besides the gigantic volcanoes. Asteroids may have crashed into the moon, gouging out huge craters. Such collisions would have sent pieces of the moon, and the asteroid, flying out into space. These particles, in turn, may have become part of the ring around earth.

Believers in the "ring" theory point out that there is evidence for the idea. Certainly there are volcanic craters on the moon, and collision craters as well. Furthermore, small, strange, glass-like rods, dumbbells, spheres and buttons have been found at various locations on earth's surface. These curiously shaped black objects are called tektites; the name comes from a Greek word that means "molten." Many scientists believe that when asteroids crashed into the moon, they generated enough heat to melt the rocks there, and tektites are chunks of that melted rock. In other words, tektites may be pieces of the moon—and they may have been suspended in a ring around earth before falling to earth's surface.

On the other hand, tektites may have been produced on earth itself. There were no doubt several periods in earth's history when there were severe lightning storms. If lightning struck sand and gravel, it could have melted those materials.

Scientists have studied tektites carefully, trying to learn what they are made of. Are they made of earth materials, or lunar matter? The answer is far from final. In some tektites the proportions of such materials as aluminum, calcium, sodium and titanium are very much like the proportions found in lunar rocks. In other cases, the proportions are more like those found in earth rocks.

People may disagree about the source of the par-

ticles that made up the ring around earth. And, of course, no one knows for certain that there ever was a ring. But the "ring" theory remains of great interest to many scientists. It provides a good explanation for the disappearance, 65 million years ago, of certain creatures and plants. It also explains why other plants and animals were able to survive into the Cenozoic Era.

During earth's long history, there may have been several occasions when it had rings. Perhaps rings are normal formations that develop as a planet forms from interstellar dust. The rings that presently surround Saturn give support to such an idea.

Just as earth may have had rings at several times in the past, it may have rings around it in the future.

The distance between earth and the moon changes. For millenia the moon moves away from earth; then it moves closer. Finally, after millions of years, the moon will be much closer to us than it is now. The force of earth's gravitation on the near side of the moon will be much greater than the force on the far side. The difference will be so great that the moon will be pulled apart—it will shatter into dust and other small particles. They will fly out into space. Eventually these particles could form into a ring around the earth. Once again winters on our planet would become bitterly cold—colder than most plants and animals could endure. And once again, many forms of life would be eliminated; only a few would survive. That, of course, would be the scenario only if earth were still here. Perhaps long before that can happen our planet will be swallowed up by the sun as it expands into the solar system.

8/
The Last Word

As you have seen for yourself, there is no last word right now about the downfall of the dinosaurs. Their disappearance remains a fascinating mystery that scientists will continue to explore.

There is very little evidence to work with—just the fossil remains of animals and plants, and the rock layers that paleontologists have learned to read much as you read the pages of a book. This is why any discovery—for example, iridium in the clays of Gubbio—is very exciting. Each discovery

stimulates new lines of investigation, and challenges scientists to explain the finding.

The earth calamity of 65 million years ago may have been the explosion of a nearby superstar, or a collision with an asteroid, or a rain of tektites. Or it may have been something entirely different.

Paleontologists continue their investigations. They are excavating in many parts of the world, searching for additional fossils, and very likely they will find fossils of creatures as yet unknown. Such fossils could provide important information about conditions at the end of the Cretaceous Period.

Through the decades paleontologists have learned much about how dinosaurs came into existence, and about how they developed and flourished for 140 million years. Why they disappeared so suddenly remains the big question. Perhaps in the near future paleontologists will be able to determine which of the theories you've been reading about is correct. Or they may find clues that point toward an entirely different explanation.

It's a mystery waiting to be solved.

For Further Reading

Aliki. *Digging Up Dinosaurs.* Crowell, 1981.

Aliki. *Fossils Tell of Long Ago.* Crowell, 1972.

Aliki. *My Visit to the Dinosaurs.* Crowell, 1969.

Colbert, Edwin H. *The Dinosaur World.* Stravon Edition Press, 1977.

Colbert, Edwin H. *The Year of the Dinosaur.* Scribner's, 1977.

Darling, Lois and Louis. *Before and After Dinosaurs.* Morrow, 1959.

Desmond, Adrian J. *Hot Blooded Dinosaurs.* Dial, 1976.

Geis, Darlene. *Dinosaurs and Other Prehistoric Reptiles.* Grosset, 1959.

Jackson, Kathryn. *Dinosaurs.* National Geographic Society, 1972.

Parish, Peggy. *Dinosaur Time.* Harper & Row, 1974.

Sattler, Helen Roney. *Dinosaurs of North America.* Lothrop, 1981.

Selsam, Millicent. *Tyrannosaurus Rex.* Harper & Row, 1978.

INDEX